TEACHING THINKING
Pocketbook

By Anne de A'Echevarria & Ian Patience

Cartoons:
Phil Hailstone

Published by:

Teachers' Pocketbooks
Laurel House, Station Approach,
Alresford, Hampshire SO24 9JH, UK
Tel: +44 (0)1962 735573
Fax: +44 (0)1962 733637
E-mail: sales@teacherspocketbooks.co.uk
Website: www.teacherspocketbooks.co.uk

*Teachers' Pocketbooks is an imprint of
Management Pocketbooks Ltd.*

Series Editor – Linda Edge.

This edition published 2008.
Reprinted 2009, 2011, 2012, 2014.

ISBN 978 1 903776 86 5
E-book ISBN 978 1 908284 96 9

British Library Cataloguing-in-Publication
Data – A catalogue record for this book is
available from the British Library.

Design, typesetting and graphics by Efex Ltd.
Printed in UK.

Contents

Foreword

We are living in the 'information age'. We are told that the disenfranchised of the 21st century will be those who have no strategies for coping with the ever-increasing bombardment of information that assaults us via our televisions, radios and mobile phones, or the flood of information that we have at our fingertips via the internet.

I consider myself ICT literate, but would my students ever use the words 'bombardment', 'assaulted' or 'flood' to describe what is happening? Would you? If it's all you've ever known it probably doesn't occur to you to welcome it or see it as a problem – most students find it exciting. In the time it takes you or me to get up and travel to work, a typical student has sent or received 20 texts, downloaded tunes onto their MP3 player, chatted online to their friends – both real and virtual – and swapped a few movie clips via their mobile phones. But despite their technological fluency – or perhaps because of it, they also struggle.

What strategies are they developing to screen all that incoming information; to discriminate between the valuable, the not so valuable, and the downright harmful? How do they know what, or who, they can trust?

Foreword

Many students have the skills to access information, but beyond lapping up information as entertainment, they do not yet have the skills they need to flourish in the 'information age'. They can communicate online, but not collaborate; they lack a critical approach to information – all is of equal worth; and living life at the pace that they do, being asked to slow down, to move back into first gear in order to think hard about what, how and why they are learning – this is effortful; they do not, in any case, have a language for doing so.

If you recognise any of the above in your students, as we do in ours, then this book is for you. It can help you to develop learners across the age and ability range who value good thinking and want to think well. It can't provide all the answers, but it describes an approach to teaching thinking that has proved successful in helping students overcome some of the problems we've outlined – problems which act as barriers to progress and development, not only across the curriculum, but also in everyday life. In our view, there has never been a more crucial time to infuse the teaching of thinking across the curriculum.

Introduction

 Processing Information

 Reasoning

 Inquiry

 Creative Thinking

 Evaluation

 The Thinking Lesson

Introduction

Can thinking be taught?

Thinking, like climbing, can be done well or poorly. There are the experts whose thinking takes them to academic, artistic and technological heights; the proficient, whose thinking helps them negotiate life's ups and downs; and the novices, who are fortunate if they escape injury on the stairs.

Happily, novice thinkers can become more expert because thinking skills, like climbing skills, can be learned, practised and improved.

Who can benefit?

As we develop our ability to think, we improve our capacity to learn. This is one definition of intelligence.

Some students have benefited from the kind of stimulating and supportive environment – particularly important in the early years – that promotes cognitive development. Teaching thinking will accelerate that development still further.

Other students have been less fortunate. For these students 'catching up' requires intervention and this is what 'teaching thinking' aims to do – to actively intervene in students' cognitive development, changing the way they think and learn.

Regardless of our age, perceived ability or background, we can all improve our thinking with encouragement, guidance and practice.

Thinking – one skill … or many?

Expert thinkers will tell you that their best ideas come in a flash. They don't laboriously assemble their thoughts like pieces of kit and they don't follow set plans to construct their amazing 'mental models'. Thinking at this level is seamless – you can't see the joins.

Novices may say the same, but there will often be a difference in the quality of the outcome. The novice's 'model' may bear only a patchy resemblance to reality, parts may be missing and those present only just hanging together…and the novice may see it as flawless!

To help novice thinkers, we have found it useful to break down the art of thinking into sub-skills that can be worked on and improved over time. We are aware that this may be seen as a simplification of the wonderfully complex thing that thinking is, into a mechanistic means to an end that ignores the mysteries of silent musing, unconscious thought and insight. It is important to keep sight of this criticism and give our students time to experience and reflect on these other dimensions of thinking which are less easily articulated and, therefore, all too often ignored.

Questions, bloomin' questions

Thinking has been sub-divided and classified in different ways for different purposes. In the 1950's Benjamin Bloom identified different orders of questions that led to different levels of thinking. Bloom's taxonomy is shown below:

Levels of thinking	Question cues
Knowledge: recall information	State, identify, list
Comprehension: make sense of ideas	Explain, describe, illustrate
Application: apply understanding in new contexts	Apply, solve, predict, infer
Analysis: identify structures and patterns	List component parts, identify cause and effect, distinguish between irrelevant/relevant, compare and contrast
Synthesis: combine ideas to make something new	Generalise, summarise, design, hypothesise, invent, create, compose
Evaluation: make judgements based on reasoned argument	Give arguments for and against, develop criteria, assess, judge, prioritise

Questions, bloomin' questions

Bloom found that over 80% of teacher questions required students to respond only at the simplest 'recall of knowledge' level.

The value of Bloom's taxonomy is that it can help you to see the connection between the sorts of questions you ask and the level of thinking they require of your students. It can help you to plan a lesson or series of lessons based on increasingly higher order questioning. For example:

- *'Who invented the light bulb?'* (identify)
- *'Can you explain how it works?'* (describe/explain)
- *'What was the impact of this invention?'* (analyse)
- *'Was it the most significant of the period?'* (compare and contrast; evaluate)

PRICE taxonomy

An alternative taxonomy organises thinking skills into five categories: **PRICE**. Unlike Bloom, there is no implied hierarchy and there is 'spill over' between categories: Creative thinking involves Evaluation, and Inquiry involves Reasoning.

Processing information — Locate/collect information; sort and classify; sequence; compare and contrast; identify part/whole relationships.

Reasoning — Give reasons; draw inferences/make deductions; see relationships; explain; make informed decisions.

Inquiry — Ask questions/define problems; plan/gather data; predict outcomes/consequences; draw/test conclusions.

Creative thinking — Generate/develop ideas; suggest hypotheses; imagine.

Evaluation — Set and use criteria; make judgements.

In its favour, PRICE is easy to remember and relates well to the types of lessons you are likely to teach. Progression and differentiation are characterised less by the *type* of thinking skill involved and more by the context, subject matter and degree of support required. (For more on teaching for progression see p.103.)

Six principles for teaching thinking

No matter which thinking skills you want to focus on with your students, or what strategies you use, a teaching thinking lesson will be characterised by six key principles. The lesson will be:

1. Active

Try to give your students the opportunity to explore ideas using a variety of thinking tools that take account of different learning styles.

2. Meaningful

A meaningful lesson will be engaging and memorable. Try to make a clear link between the skill focus of the lesson and its usefulness in everyday life.

3. Challenging

A challenging lesson will change minds. The idea is to present your students with a cognitive challenge that is not so great as to overwhelm, but not so slight that it is boring. Students will be working at the edge of their understanding.

Six principles for teaching thinking

4. Collaborative

We learn from others, so collaboration makes sense. Students will be working in small groups using their own approaches. Your role is to support them as they explore their differences of opinion and interpretation.

5. Mediated

Challenge your students to think as much as possible for themselves. Try to take on the role of guide and adviser, rather than that of expert or guru.

6. Reflective

At various points in the lesson, learners think about their thinking. Your role is to ask questions that will help your students to figure out what they have learned, how they learned it and where it might be useful in the future.

Teaching thinking toolbox

The next five sections of this Pocketbook form a toolbox of practical strategies that you can use to develop your students' thinking skills. The 'thinking tools' are versatile – we've seen the same tool used effectively in many subject contexts at every stage between Reception and Degree Level – and they are fun. Like all tools, their skilful use comes with practice. Aim to use each tool several times, adapting to suit the needs and abilities of learners and the requirements of the curriculum.

All of the suggested activities will involve students in using and combining a range of different thinking skills. Sometimes, though, it is helpful to focus attention on one particular skill, such as evaluation or reasoning, if this is a particular area of difficulty for your students.

Each of the following sections takes a 'troubleshooting' approach. The types of thinking that students typically struggle with are matched with 'thinking tools' that can be used to help them overcome these particular areas of difficulty. The troubleshooting approach will help you to select the most effective tool for the job.

Tools for better thinking

The value of thinking tools is that:

- They introduce and guide students through the skilful practice of required thinking
- They make thinking processes visible and explicit
- They slow down the thinking
- They provide a visible record of thinking processes for teachers and learners to reflect on and discuss

Thinking tools are not the 'new worksheets'; emphasis is on the thinking process. You can begin to remove the tools when your students begin to demonstrate confidence with a particular thinking process, eg 'decision making' or 'evaluation'.

Troubleshooting

Here are five of the most common 'thinking problems' that students face, according to teacher surveys. As you can see, they relate closely to the **PRICE** taxonomy.

Problem 1 (Page 20)

Processing Information

Struggles to order and organise new information and therefore to recall it.

Problem 2 (Page 40)

Reasoning

Has trouble forming an opinion and justifying a view; tends to be uncritical of ideas and information.

Problem 3 (Page 60)

Inquiry

Finds it hard to initiate and sustain an independent project or inquiry.

Problem 4 (Page 77)

Creative Thinking

Struggles to come up with or develop ideas.

Problem 5 (Page 88)

Evaluation

Evaluation is superficial; little awareness of the criteria they're using to make judgements.

Introduction

 Processing Information

 Reasoning

 Inquiry

 Creative Thinking

 Evaluation

 The Thinking Lesson

Processing Information

Where's the problem?

> *Struggles to order and organise new information and therefore to recall it.*

Do any of your students feel overwhelmed when faced with a body of new information, whether facts, figures or ideas? If so, there are thinking tools in this section specifically designed to help them process that information more effectively by ordering and organising it so that it becomes more manageable and more memorable. These tools are:

- Odd One Out
- Knowledge Mapping
- Parts and Wholes
- Collective Memory

Thinking tool: Odd One Out

Asking students to pick the 'odd one out' from a set of words or pictures encourages them to think about the characteristics of things. Understanding how one phenomenon is **similar** or **different** from another helps you to describe it clearly and associate it with other important, related information. It is fundamental to classification.

Odd One Out combines the fun and simplicity of a party game with the potential to stimulate high order thinking in students at every age and stage of development.

What would you say the odd one out is here? (Remember: there is always more than one possible answer!)

And the odd one out here?

Odd One Out instructions

1. Distribute sets of key words from the topic you are teaching. You could also use pictures, objects or numbers.
2. Tell your students that each set has an odd one out and that they have to decide what it is.
3. Encourage 'full answers' in which students justify their selection, explaining what the items have in common and what differs in the odd one out.

You could offer sets of three, or four, or even a 3x3 grid where students try to find and justify an odd one out in any row, column or diagonal.

plastic
wood
metal

materials in D&T

circle
area
circumference
diameter

geometry in maths

Odd One Out teaching tips

You will find that your students engage enthusiastically with this strategy. The less able will enjoy identifying the more obvious odd ones out and the more able will search for ways to make each one of the items the exception. Your task will be to channel this enthusiasm towards the creation of fully justified answers that are received critically by the class. Here are some variants:

- Get students to brainstorm as many key words as they can, associated with the topic they are studying or have just finished. Number the words they come up with. Then complete some whole-class quick-fire rounds, eg: *'1, 8, 13 – which is the odd one out?'* This makes an excellent starter or plenary activity
- Once students have identified an odd one out, ask them to add another word to the set, whilst keeping the same odd one out
- Challenge students to create their own sets and exchange with another group

Odd One Out teaching tips (continued)

Use a frame such as this one, showing a maths example, to ensure that students give reasons for the similarities and differences they find.

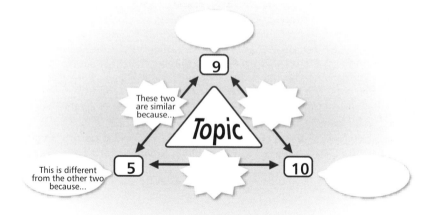

Odd One Out – talking about thinking

Provide students with the language they will need to express their ideas clearly:

> **same/similar/share** **different /distinct/degree** **characteristics/properties**
> **category/class** **categorise/classify** **compare/contrast**

You could also offer them a script to scaffold their responses, for example:

'_____ is similar to _____ because _____, but _____ is different from the

other two because _____.'

Encourage students to **make connections**, **generalise** and **see a bigger picture** with regard to the value of being able to make careful comparisons and distinctions.

Thinking tool: Knowledge Mapping

Grouping and separating similar and dissimilar items is a fundamental function of the human mind. Knowledge Mapping challenges students to **classify information hierarchically**, moving from a central 'organising' idea via connectors to sub-sets.

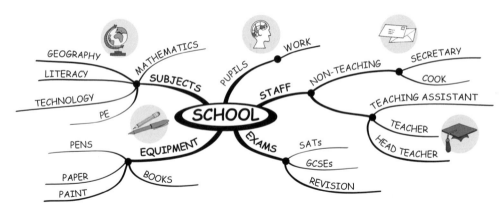

Knowledge Mapping instructions

If your students are interested in a topic, they will want to map their knowledge of it. We have seen reception stage children collaborating on mapping photographs of themselves; 'A' Level students individually mapping a Physics module; and teachers mapping their courses. We always encourage individual expression while providing the following recommendations:

1 Use landscape format.

2 Place the organising idea or topic in the centre of the paper.

3 Chunk your information into 4 or 5 major categories, choosing key words (nouns) to label each category.

4 These key words radiate from the centre.

5 Each category can then be sub-divided as many times as necessary. Make this memorable by using:
- Thick lines to thin lines and big letters to little letters
- Colours for different sub-sections
- Colourful supporting images or symbols.

Knowledge Mapping teaching tips

- Help students to see the value of Knowledge Mapping by modelling the process yourself with an everyday topic and making explicit how it will help their learning

- Demonstrate how personalising a knowledge map with unusual fonts, layouts and illuminations is both enjoyable and helpful because it aids memory and recall

- Ask students to read back and explain their knowledge maps to a partner – as well as embedding new learning and aiding recall, this also helps students to reinterpret the information in linear form once more as a precursor to any extended writing

- Use Knowledge Mapping at the beginning of a topic to uncover what students already know, or at the end of a topic to help them reflect on what they have learned and to develop their own overview or 'big picture' of the topic

- As a further revision technique, students can traffic light what they are confident about (highlight in green), what needs more work (amber), and what they still need support with (red) prior to a test or exam

Knowledge Mapping – talking about thinking

Provide students with the language to talk about what they have learned and how they went about constructing their knowledge maps:

| similar | category | connection | memorise | big picture |
| different | classify | organise | remember | |

- Could they have organised their knowledge map differently?
- Were some facts or ideas harder to classify than others?

Tell stories and use analogies to encourage students to make connections, generalise and see a bigger picture with regard to the value of being able to process information and use the Knowledge Mapping technique.

- *'Where else in school would Knowledge Mapping be useful?'*
- *'Is learning to manage information effectively useful for everyday life?'*

Thinking tool: Parts and Wholes

Whenever we plan, we think about parts and wholes because, whether we are planning an outing, a meal or a story, we have to make sure that the equipment, ingredients, characters and settings suit our purpose, ie that the parts make up an effective whole. The Parts and Wholes tool helps to focus attention on this point and is a memorable way of helping students to see the value of analysing part/whole relationships.

Your students will have great fun debating the inclusion or exclusion of each 'part' on offer and envisaging the final result, and you will enjoy their total engagement in applying the terms and concepts that are at the heart of your topic.

The nature of the planning task will depend on your topic. Our students have designed animals to suit particular environments, paintings for set locations and music for given occasions. We used the example on the next page as part of a programme to help students revise for exams.

Parts and Wholes instructions

1. Explain to your students that they are going to plan the perfect 'test-buster'. In threes, they will have to explore a list of attributes and agree on just six that will combine to create the perfect student for examination success. They will then draw their 'test-buster', making each attribute clear in the drawing.

2. Hand out the list (make sure some of the attributes are inappropriate and include many that will vie for inclusion to make the effective 'whole'), encourage questions for clarification and then begin the planning.

3. Listen-in to group discussions and make a note of any dialogue that will inform the debrief that follows.

4. When groups have chosen their six attributes, provide drawing materials and prepare to be surprised by unexpected talents in humour and art.

5. Have each group name their 'test buster' and present him or her to the class, with an explanation of how the parts work together to form an effective whole.

Possible attributes of a 'test-buster'

Honest
Can think ahead
Well organised
Good memory
Good self-knowledge
Able to keep secrets
Been on TV
Takes risks
Good negotiator
Knows where to go for help
Good sense of humour
Knows how to stay healthy
Optimistic
Tough
Mischievous
Loyal
Good thinker
Obedient
Curious
Flexible
Can juggle
Wears glasses
Self-confident
Knows their stuff
Self-disciplined
Decisive
Physically fit
Gives people what they want
Follows instructions
Motivated

Parts and Wholes teaching tips

Launch the activity by asking the whole class for examples of successful events or products. What makes them good? Choose one that you know is of interest and collect reasons why it might be really good. One group of students enjoyed suggesting a host of attributes for a successful mobile phone that included: good reception, a colourful shell, good games, and – more imaginatively – a heart rate monitor, thermometer and electric shaver!

From the list, which six would they choose for their phone?
And which six would make the phone popular with the over 60s?

Parts and Wholes requires teamwork: students must share their knowledge and skills and collaborate effectively on their plan. Since team performance depends on individuals coordinating different contributions for the good of the 'whole', this tool is perfect for introducing and revisiting ideas about unity in diversity and joint effort.

Parts and Wholes – talking about thinking

In the course of the lesson and in the plenary, your students may find the following words useful:

part	detail	synthesise	purpose	collaboration
whole	analyse	plan	function	complementary
big picture	prioritise	design	effective	cooperation

- *'What is it about those attributes that appear in all the different 'test-busters'?'*
- *'Were some attributes harder to decide on than others?'*

Encourage your students to talk about times, both in and out of school, when a better view of the 'big picture' would have been helpful:

- *'Where else in school and in adult life could 'Parts and Wholes' be used?'*
- *'What are the 'parts and wholes' of your favourite subjects?'*
- *'How well did you work together?'*
- *'What makes for effective teamwork?'*

Thinking tool: Collective Memory

Collective Memory is a one of the best ways of encouraging your students to think about how they take in and process information and about how to work effectively as a team.

The aim is for your students to cooperate in teams of four or five, each team operating as a 'human photocopier', reproducing information as accurately as possible. The information can be an image, map, diagram, body of text, or a combination of these and should represent an important element of the curriculum that you would like them to remember.

Collective Memory spotlights teamwork and the different ways in which individuals remember, recall and represent information. With all age groups, the strategy is guaranteed to create a buzz of excitement. It is pacy, it engages everyone and there is an element of competition between teams that intensifies the concentration of individuals engaged in memorising and recalling the data. It's all good fun but beware: too much pressure could cause the odd 'photocopier' to blow up!

Collective Memory instructions

1. Connect the ideas of effective teamwork and accurate memory and recall to previous work. Introduce the idea of working together as human photocopiers.

2. Organise teams of four (or five) students. Each team member adopts a number from 1 to 4 (or 5).

3. Place the map or diagram to be 'copied' under a sheet of paper so you can reveal it easily to a small group without it being seen by the others, eg on a flip chart turned away from the class.

4. Explain that you will call up all the number 1s and they will have 10 seconds to 'scan' and memorise the information. They will return to their teams and begin the process of reproducing it as exactly as possible. Then you will call up the 2s, then the 3s, and then the 4s. Everyone will get (at least) 3 turns.

5. Allow time at the beginning for teams to plan how they will go about the task and again half-way through for them to review and modify their approach.

6. Start the 'photocopiers'.

Collective Memory teaching tips

Launch the activity by asking your students to suggest the benefits of having a 'photographic memory', eg exam success and never losing one's way. Tell them you are going to help them improve their memory.

If you have done work on 'Parts and Wholes' (page 30) you can refer to this, reminding students that understanding how detail relates to an overarching structure helps memory and recall.

Ensure that the information to be 'copied' is important to your current topic and that it has a clear structure. There should be sufficient detail to challenge but not overwhelm the students.

Aim to balance the excitement associated with teamwork, time limits and competition with the time, concentration and care required for good memory and recall.

Collective Memory – talking about thinking

Useful words in the debrief may be:

similar	part	memory	challenge	image
different	whole	recall	support	text
identical	big picture	strategy	communication	meaning

- *'How did you do that task as an individual? ...As a team?'*
- *'How did your approach change in the course of the activity?'*
- *'What advice would you give to another team new to this strategy?'*
- *'Why do we remember some things but forget others?'*
- *'How is your memory and recall different from a photocopier?'*

Reasoning

Where's the problem?

Has trouble forming an opinion and justifying a view; tends to be uncritical of ideas and information.

The thinking tools in this section are specifically designed to help students practise and develop the **skill of reasoning**:

- Opinion Line
  (giving reasons for opinions and
  actions; arguing your case)

- Concept Line
  (making distinctions)

- Concept Mapping
  (making connections; seeing relationships)

But first, let's take a general look at what we mean by 'reasoned argument'.

Learning to argue

It is worth making a distinction between a **quarrel** and a **reasoned argument**. In a quarrel, a person aims to overpower another with insults and harsh words, while in a reasoned argument a person aims to persuade another with reasons and conclusions. Because argument is so important to a reliable understanding of the world, it is well worth your while helping students to argue well. The first step is to be clear about what an argument is and isn't:

- An argument seeks to *persuade* us to accept something as fact that we didn't previously hold to be so

- An argument has one or more *reasons* that support a *conclusion*

$$Argument = \begin{array}{c} conclusion\ (C) \\ + \\ reasons\ (R) \end{array}$$

'I think you should take a raincoat (C) because the sky is looking black (R),' **is** an argument.

'I think you should take a raincoat (C), the one with the hood,' **is not** an argument because there is no given reason. It is simply an assertion.

Evaluating arguments

When students have learned to **identify** an argument, they can then learn to **evaluate** how good it is. Helping your students to evaluate arguments will help them to deal critically with the daily barrage of views that comes their way in everyday life and though the media.

Arguments can be valid or invalid, strong or weak, depending on the quality of the logic, the credibility of the evidence and the assumptions that lie hidden behind the reasons and the effort to persuade.

The argument, *'You should take a raincoat because the sky is looking black,'* may appear very weak indeed if:

- You are aware that it is after sunset (alternative reason for a darkening sky)
- The arguer has poor eyesight (unreliable source of evidence)
- You would quite enjoy getting soaked to the skin because it hasn't rained for weeks (mistaken assumption that getting wet is always bad)

Hare-brained logic

Arguments can move you from what you already know to be true to a new understanding that you weren't aware of. However, reliable evidence doesn't always lead to true conclusions. If the logic is poor, conclusions can be false.

For instance, you will agree with me that all rabbits eat carrots and also that your neighbour eats carrots, but would you be happy with my conclusion that your neighbour is therefore a rabbit?

Sometimes conclusions are false because although the stated reasons are true, there may be another idea, crucial to the argument, which is **un**stated and **un**true.

For instance, you might say, *'That lion looks like my cat and my cat enjoys a good cuddle, so I'll just hop over this fence and give that lion a cuddle'* – a decision you might regret because of that underlying, and sadly mistaken, assumption that the lion shares your cat's behaviours.

Focusing on improving reasoning will inevitably involve you in helping your students uncover their mistaken assumptions.

Thinking tool: Opinion Line

Opinion Line is an effective tool for stimulating **the expression, challenge, review and refinement of opinions**. It will give students the opportunity to:

- Show (literally) where they stand on an issue
- See the spread of opinion in the class
- Think critically about their own and others' views
- Demonstrate changes in opinion through physical movement

Opinion Line is useful in changing the dynamic of a lesson because it involves students in getting out of their seats, moving around the room and engaging each other in discussion. So, if your students are 'going to sleep', turn your content into an issue, make a contentious statement and introduce an opinion line.

Opinion Line instructions

① Formulate a statement that expresses a point of view relating to your current topic. It should be bold and contentious so that it's likely to stir the feelings of everyone in the class. An example might be: *'People who damage their own health should pay the cost of their own treatment'*.

② Clear a space at the side, or across the centre of your classroom that will serve as a line where students can stand shoulder to shoulder. You can lay a rope on the floor or fix paper tape to the wall.

③ Mark one end with a sign saying 'Agree Strongly' and the other end with 'Disagree Strongly'.

④ Explain that you are going to give them an opinion about an issue and that you are interested in their opinions on the matter. When they have had time to think about the statement, ask them to stand on the opinion line at a point that shows how much they agree or disagree.

Opinion Line instructions (continued)

⑤ Encourage students to share their views with others close to them on the line, perhaps using 'exploratory talk prompt cards' (see page 112). They should change places if appropriate.

⑥ Deeper, paired discussion can be stimulated if you split the line at the mid-point and 'slide' one half over the other so that students with more extreme and more moderate views will exchange ideas.

Pairs in discussion

Opinion Line teaching tips

Launch by using a light-hearted example, eg *'Red Riding Hood was a fool to go into the woods alone'*, or *'Ignorance is bliss'*. The aim at this stage is for your students to feel at ease with standing on the line and sharing their views with one another and with the whole class. Remind them there are no right/wrong answers and that they should express *their* views rather than adopting those of their friends.

You might wish to encourage paired discussion (see instruction 6) to aim for consensus. This may involve them re-writing the original statement so that they can both agree, eg *'People who damage their own health should be made to pay the cost of their treatment...**if they can afford it**'*.

Once your students are happy to share their opinions – and then to challenge and justify them – they may be ready to explore the subject of 'reasoned argument' (pages 41-43) in some detail.

Opinion Line – talking about thinking

Words that might help in the course of the activity and in the plenary are:

fact	opinion	agree	disagree	example
reason	persuade	convince	exception	conclusion
evidence	reliable	assumption	if/then	argument

Questions that can help to develop students' thinking might include:

- *'How might someone argue against that opinion?'*
- *'If you have changed your opinion, why?'*
- *'What is the difference between a fact and an opinion?'*
- *'Is that a good argument for...? Is that a good argument against...?'*
- *'What are you assuming when you argue that?'*
- *'Is it always easy/right to express your opinion?'*

Thinking tool: Concept Line

Concept lines can be used to deepen students' understanding of a concept that lies at the heart of a given topic or lesson.

Concepts are never straightforward and pure. One concept tends to merge into another; what is 'good' seems to shade into what is 'bad' as white shades into black. Concept lines help students to explore these grey areas and to develop their reasoning skills at the same time.

A concept line is 'drawn' between a particular concept and its opposite, eg 'fair/unfair', 'courage/not courage' or 'art/not art'. Students position a set of possible 'examples' (see next page) of the concept in question along this line.

courage   **not courage**

Concept to be explored: COURAGE

1 Standing up to a bully alone when you know that he is stronger than you and has hurt other people badly.

2 Being addicted to the scariest roller-coaster rides.

3 Diving into a river to save someone from drowning. You are a very poor swimmer.

4 Overcoming shyness and embarrassment by taking a pill.

5 Coping well with a serious illness.

6 Stopping someone from bullying another person but you are a lot stronger than both of them.

7 Getting a thrill from running across the tracks just before a train goes by.

8 Not diving into a river to save someone from drowning. You are a very poor swimmer.

9 Owning up when you have done something wrong.

10 Fighting your enemies.

Concept Line instructions

1 Give each group of students an A3 concept line template, or simply get them to draw a concept line on a sheet of paper and label either end with the concepts you have chosen. Also distribute a set of numbered 'example' cards.

2 Ask each group to look at each example in turn and place it somewhere on the line, between the two extremes.

3 Warn them that you will be asking them to explain and justify their placements. In your set of examples make sure you include:

- Some that are definitely instances of the concept in question
- Some that are definitely not instances of the concept in question
- Some from the 'grey area' where students will be less certain, will tend to disagree with each other, will have to consider what others say and may change their minds as the discussion proceeds. In the process, they will be encouraged to justify their viewpoints, make distinctions, and develop criteria upon which to base their judgements

Concept Line – talking about thinking

Here are some 'thinking words' that you might introduce to help your students express their ideas clearly:

explain	reason	example	opinion	alternative	infer
assume	opposite	difference/distinction	criteria	definition	rule

Help the class to make a list of the criteria they've used to reach their decisions and to feel their way towards a definition of the key concept.

- *'What criteria have you used to decide that this statement is an example of courage whereas that one is not?'*
- *'So what does it mean to be courageous?'*

Thinking tool: Concept Mapping

A concept map aims to show the **connections** that a student sees between different concepts – usually the key terms from a particular topic or series of lessons. These could be:

- Subject specific terms
- Causes of a key event
- Motives
- Specific things, people or events
- Emotions
- Actions
- A combination of the above

Concept maps will help reinforce understanding of these key terms and, in particular, will help students analyse and gain a deeper understanding of the overall structure of a topic.

Concept Mapping instructions for teachers

Organise your students into groups of three or four and provide each group with:

- A set of Concept Cards (see page 50) showing the key terms to be mapped. (When students are thinking about their concept map, it is important for them to be able to manipulate physically the concept labels.)
- A sheet of paper on which to arrange the cards – large enough to permit plenty of space between the cards – and some glue.

Decide on the key question that will be the focus of the concept map, eg *'What caused the Second World War?'* or *'What makes a good holiday?'*

Concept Mapping instructions for students

1. Sort through the cards and put to one side any that have a term you don't know or that you think are not related to any other term.

2. Put the remaining cards on the sheet of paper and arrange them in a way that makes sense to you. Terms you see as related should be kept fairly close together, but leave space between even the closest cards.

3. When you are satisfied with your arrangement, stick the cards to the sheet.

4. Draw lines between the terms you see to be related.

5. Write on each line why you think they are related.

6. If you put any cards to one side at the start, go back to these and see if you now want to add any to the map.

Concept Mapping teaching tips

Introduce by modelling one in front of the class using a simple, familiar topic, eg *'What makes a good holiday?'* Allow students to hear you working aloud and invite them to help you, reducing their statements to single words, so *'You need money to buy things like food and presents'* becomes 'money', 'food' and 'presents'.

Concept Map
What makes a good holiday?

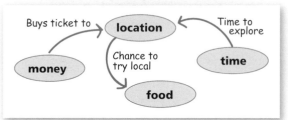

Pick any two words and ask students to suggest how they are linked. Join the words with an arrow and write in the link. Continue until all the words are linked.

Help students realise that there is no single, correct answer to the task and that there is often more than one appropriate link between a pair of concepts.

Concept Mapping teaching tips (continued)

You can change the basic procedure to suit the topic, your purpose and the age and experience of your students. The examples below demonstrate how versatile the strategy can be, both for developing students' understanding and as a means of formative/summative assessment for the teacher:

- Use to help students understand the reasons for a lesson
- Can your students see how one topic relates to another?
- Do your students understand which concepts are the key ones?
- Use to identify changes in relations that students perceive between concepts
- Use to help students link a new concept into their ideas

Concept Mapping – talking about thinking

In the course of the lesson and in the plenary, your students may find the following words useful:

big picture/detail   **connections**   **explanation**   **reason**   **understanding**

You could ask your class to create a concept map using some of the words above as a way of helping them to explore the value of the Concept Mapping strategy:

'Can all words be connected by a linking idea?' Challenge your students to try and come up with any two words that *cannot* be connected. No student has ever managed in our experience, but they enjoy trying to outwit each other!

Introduction

 Processing
Information

 Reasoning

 Inquiry

 Creative
Thinking

 Evaluation

 The Thinking
Lesson

Inquiry

Where's the problem?

> *Finds it hard to initiate and sustain an independent project or inquiry.*

If your students struggle with processing information, reasoning, creativity and evaluation, then they will certainly struggle with inquiry. This is because inquiry draws on and combines all of the other thinking skills. It also demands more in the way of sustained effort. Inquiries can flounder due to three common problems:

- Your students aren't motivated by the idea of inquiry: they just don't see the point of all that study because the topic appears to have nothing to do with their interests or lives

- The inquiry is too 'open': it lacks a clearly explained structure that will support the thinking of your novice inquirers

- The inquiry is too 'closed': the topic, questions, data, method and even the outcomes have been predetermined so that students lack any sense of ownership or excitement

Closed, framed or open?

The ultimate aim is for students to conduct their own, independent inquiries. To support this, use a combination of the inquiry modes shown here, 'opening up' or 'closing down' according to the needs of your students.

Closed	**Framed**	**Open**
Limited range of skills		*Complete range of skills*
Teacher selects: • Topic • Questions • Data and structure	Teacher encourages, mediates, and models	Students select: • Topic • Questions • Data, tools and structure
…outcome predetermined	Students acquire the tools and culture of inquiry	..and arrive at their own conclusions

For example, you might start in a closed way, choosing the focus, questions and resources, but enabling students to decide how to present and analyse data. Or, students could choose the focus of their inquiry but have structured guidelines on how to investigate. Offering choice gives students **ownership** of the process and raises levels of **motivation**.

The SECRET of inquiry

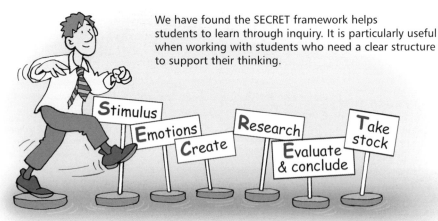

We have found the SECRET framework helps students to learn through inquiry. It is particularly useful when working with students who need a clear structure to support their thinking.

Stimulus
Emotions
Create
Research
Evaluate & conclude
Take stock

The next two pages show how each SECRET step of the inquiry process is linked to the types of thinking involved and to one or more of the tools in this book that can help students develop this type of thinking.

The SECRET framework

Inquiry - steps	Types of thinking	Thinking tools
Stimulus	• Speculate, puzzle, wonder • Make links with existing knowledge and experience • Identify issues and problems	Opinion Line (p.44) Inference Square (p.70) 3, 5, 7 (p.106) Concept Line (p.49)
Emotions	• Express feelings, identify emotions	Feelygauge (p.107)
Create	• Create questions • Devise a plan for how to investigate the issue/problem	8Q templates (p.109)
Research	• Decide type of data/evidence to be collected • Gather and organise evidence • Analyse/make sense of evidence	Knowledge Mapping (p.26) Inference Square (p.70) Concept Mapping (p.53) Odd One Out (p.21) Collective Memory (p.35)
Evaluate and conclude		
Take stock		

The SECRET framework

Inquiry - steps	Types of thinking	Thinking tools
Stimulus		
Emotions		
Create		
Research		
Evaluate and conclude	• Evaluate data/evidence • Decide whether more/different data is needed • Make reasoned conclusions/decisions	Target Board (p.94) Diamond Ranking (p.89)
Take stock	• Reflect on what has been learnt • Re-order existing knowledge • Form opinions • Generate/develop ideas for action	Skills and attitudes cards (p.121) Transfer games (p.125) Concept Mapping (p.53) Kick Cards (p.78) The Inverse (p.85)

Thinking tool: Mystery

There are two thinking tools specially designed to help your students to an understanding of what an inquiry is, how it can be structured and how they can generate questions to guide inquiries of their own. The first of these is 'Mystery', a problem-solving activity based round a given central question that is open to more than one reasonable answer.

The information or 'clues' needed to answer the question are presented on separate slips of paper that your students will **analyse**, **sort**, **sequence** and **link**. Mysteries are a good introduction to inquiry:

- They provide your students with an inquiry experience that fits neatly into one lesson
- They provide you with the opportunity to make inquiry structures and skills explicit and memorable
- They motivate. The narrative thread that runs through a mystery will successfully engage your students and they will be eager to find out more about the characters at the centre of the action and events

Mystery – instructions for making

① Identify a theme in your topic that will lend itself to inquiry or which would benefit by being 'problematised' and 'personalised' in a narrative. For example, a science project on energy might lend itself to a mystery: *'Why did Mr and Mrs Green sell their car?'*

② Make a set of 15-25 slips that provide the necessary information. Continuing with the Smith's car sale example, a set of slips might include:

- 6-7 background or context clues (eg Mrs Green's driving licence/wage slips/ pension plan/date/method for measuring CO_2 emissions)

- 4-5 actions or causes of change (eg doctor's report on Mrs Green's heart, CO_2 emissions report, visit of Greenpeace activist)

- 4-5 reactions or effects of change (eg application to join the local golf club, e-mail regarding sale of house, car sale advert)

- 2-4 red herrings to confuse. They are relevant to the theme but not to the inquiry question (eg formula for combustion, nuclear energy facts)

- 1-3 pieces of irrelevant information (eg Mr Green's favourite food)

Mystery – instructions for teaching

① Organise students into groups of four and give them the key 'mystery' question.

② Show them the information slips and explain that their task is to solve the mystery by providing a full answer to the question. Encourage them to think of a strategy for doing this.

③ Hand out the information slips and allow the students to get on with it. Some will sequence the slips into a story; others may group together those that relate to each character.

④ Hear both the conclusions and the different strategies that students have used.

⑤ If appropriate, students could then be asked to classify the information in a variety of different ways, eg into sets of background, long-term, short-term and trigger causes.

⑥ Other possibilities could involve asking students to prioritise the reasons they have found or linking the evidence in a concept map (see page 53).

Mystery teaching tips

Introduce the Mystery tool by asking, *'In real life who solves mysteries?'*.
Having established that this is typically the work of detectives, you can ask,
'How do they do this?' and draw out from your students suggestions about the
inquiry process.

Vary the level of difficulty by varying the amount,
complexity and form of the information; by
introducing all the slips at once, or distributing
them in stages.

Allow room among your pieces of
information for ambiguity and inference.
Inquiry often throws up facts that can appear
unrelated until new evidence provides the link
and the *'Ahh...now it makes sense!'* moment.

Allow questions to clarify meanings and
terminology on the slips.

Mystery – talking about thinking

Words that might help in the course of the activity and in the plenary are:

inquire	infer	plan	link/connect	probable
analyse	hypothesise	conclude	evidence	possible
sequence	predict	refine	data	certain

Encourage your students to consider the following:

- *'How did you solve the mystery?'*
- *'Is that a full answer; is there anything left unexplained?'*
- *'What assumptions/inferences have you made: are they reasonable?'*
- *'What have you learned that could help you to find answers to your own questions? What other information could be presented as a mystery?'*

Thinking tool: Inference Square

The Inference Square is a particularly effective strategy for **stimulating curiosity** and for encouraging students to take ownership of the inquiry process. It is also useful for students who tend to take information at face value, as it encourages them to:

- 'Read between the lines' – **drawing inferences** from what they see or read
- Take a more **critical approach** to the information and evidence they are using during their inquiry, therefore increasing the validity of their conclusions

Inference Square instructions

The Inference Square stimulates curiosity by starting with an intriguing source, usually a picture or photograph.

1. Organise students into groups of four and distribute the source and the Inference Square template. (See next page.)

2. Working outwards from the centre, students must respond to a series of questions that draw them into an increasingly sophisticated analysis and evaluation of the source and spur them to create inquiry questions of their own:

- *'What does this source/picture/information tell you for certain?'*
- *'What can you infer (work out) from this source?'*
- *'What does this source not tell you?'*
- *'What questions do you have?'*

Inference Square template

What **questions** do you have?

What does this source **not** tell you?

What can you **infer** from this source?

What does this source tell you for **certain**?

Inference Square teaching tips

With a more complex picture, you could overlay a grid and ask each group of students to look in detail at a different section. This tends to encourage students to look longer and 'see more' within their particular section.

Make the skill of inference more explicit and visible to your students by asking them to draw lines between facts they have recorded in the central box and the related inferences. The example is taken from an inference square on Victorian towns.

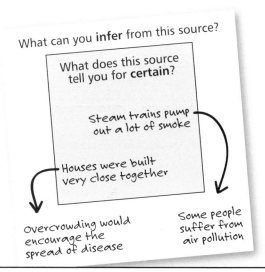

What can you **infer** from this source?

What does this source tell you for **certain**?

Steam trains pump out a lot of smoke

Houses were built very close together

Overcrowding would encourage the spread of disease

Some people suffer from air pollution

Inference Square – talking about thinking

Students will find the following words useful to help them talk about their thinking:

> fact   opinion   certain   infer/inference   hypothesis   source
> evidence   challenge   question   evaluate   useful   reliable
> connection   prove   inquire

Encourage students to explain the inferences they have made with reference
to the source:

- *'What made you think that?'*
- *'What are the clues in the source that led you to that conclusion?'*

Other talking points might include:

- *'What's the difference between giving an opinion and making an inference?'*
- *'What's the difference between imagining and making an inference?'*
- *'When might 'reading between the lines' be a useful skill to have in everyday life?'*

Creative Thinking

Creative Thinking

What's the problem?

> **Struggles to come up with or to develop ideas.**

We all have a natural capacity to imagine, think speculatively and make bold connections between ideas. However, as children grow older this capacity is often dulled, whether due to an overdose of high-stakes testing, fear of failure, anxiety or peer pressure.

The thinking tools in this section are collaborative and fun. They aim to reduce the anxiety felt by many students when faced with a creative task – an anxiety that leads them to 'play safe'. The tools are specifically designed to help students gain the confidence to think past the first 'safe' ideas they come up with and develop personally novel and innovative solutions:

- Kick Cards
- The Inverse
- Double 6

Thinking tool: Kick Cards

Kick Cards contain random words and/or pictures that can be used to **trigger fresh ideas** or **new perspectives** during problem solving.

When challenged to come up with design ideas in D&T, to write a story or poem, to produce an advert or slogan, or even to find a solution to an everyday problem, many of us find it very difficult to 'think outside the box' and move beyond safe, conventional approaches.

Kick Cards are powerful in stimulating lateral thinking. They 'kick' you out of existing unproductive patterns of thinking and on to a new track. This tool is by far the simplest of all creative techniques and can often lead to startling creative leaps.

Kick Cards instructions

Start off by summing up the issue or problem you are trying to resolve in the form of a question. This focuses your thinking. For example:

1. *What would an eye-catching hat for a fancy dress party look like?* (D&T). *How can we solve the graffiti problem?* (School council). *What would be a good slogan for a charity campaigning against child labour?* (Geography; Citizenship).

2. Select a card at random from the pack. It is important to use the first word you find. This new input will force you to look at the problem in a new way.

3. Take the word/picture you have selected and jot down any words that come to mind that describe it, or that you associate with it.

4. Use your list of words as a spring board to help you think of solutions. Try to apply each word in turn to the problem at hand.

Kick Cards example outcomes

Below are some ideas generated by secondary students using Kick Cards in response to the example questions on the previous page.

The problem	Kick Card and associated words	Possible solutions
What would an eye-catching hat for a fancy dress party look like? (D&T)	BANANA: yellow; sunny; squashed; soft; crescent moon; canoe; milkshake; healthy; monkey; tropical.	A tall cone-shaped hat like an upside down knickerbockerglory, decorated with fruit and multicoloured ice cream scoops. A moon-shaped hat decorated with stars in a soft velvety material.
What would be a good slogan for a charity campaigning against child labour? (Geography)	CAT: purring; soft; clever; curled up in front of the fire; nine lives; scratching.	Smart rug, ragged child: *think* before you buy! A cat has nine lives; a child doesn't.

Kick Cards teaching tips

You could introduce the idea of Kick Cards by modelling the technique in front of the class and allowing them to hear you working aloud. You could use one of the examples in the table on the previous page. Or, if you are feeling brave, choose a problem or task that the students themselves might be familiar with, ask a student to pick a card for you, and work 'live' with whatever card is selected!

Other techniques for generating 'random inputs' include:

- Close your eyes and point to a random place on a page of text in a magazine, newspaper or dictionary. Nouns that can be seen or touched (eg 'lighthouse', 'dog') work better than concepts (eg 'fairness')

- Make up your own list of 60 words. Look at your watch and take note of the seconds. Use this number to get the word

- Use pictures cut from various pieces of advertising material and magazines. You will often find that the ambiguity of a picture will generate even more creative ideas than just a random word input

Thinking tool: Double 6 – instructions

Double 6 uses a 6x6 template and two dice. It is a useful tool to help students **develop ideas** for a story or piece of drama and to **make connections between ideas**.

1 Pick two parameters – one for the horizontal x-axis and the other for the vertical y-axis. The example on the next page focuses on developing characters for a piece of fantasy writing using the parameters: *attractive/repulsive* and *good/evil*.

2 Each group of students has a Double 6 template and a pair of dice which they take turns to roll. Say you threw a six and a three, use the grid as a matrix and, starting at the bottom left corner, count 6 along and 3 up to find where they intersect. You will now have to create a character suggested by this grid square.

3 Keep rolling the dice for a specified period of time or until you have brainstormed as many characters as you need. You can then begin to create possible links or relationships between them.

Double 6 template

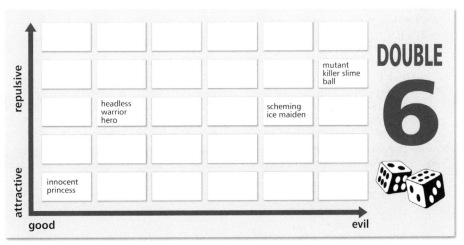

For brainstorming different settings, possible parameters might include *wet*/*dry*;
hot/*cold* or *flat*/*mountainous*.

A different Double 6 example

You can also use a version of Double 6 for finding **connections between key words** from a particular topic:

1 Fill all the Double 6 grid spaces with the key words – you could do this as a whole class activity to allow for a bit of judicious editing on your part.

2 Each group of students has a filled template and a pair of dice which they roll twice to select two words. Now think up as many connections as you can between the two words.

As an alternative, you might prefer to use a 3-sided spinner and a 3x3 grid with just nine key words for students to focus on.

Thinking tool: The Inverse – instructions

'The Inverse' is another tool for **generating ideas**. Students of all ages love the freedom to think outside the box and are amazed at the creative ideas it triggers.

1. Start off by summing up the issue or problem you are trying to resolve in the form of a question, eg *'How can we solve the school graffiti problem?'*

2. Reformulate the question so that it becomes negative, eg *'How can we encourage graffiti and vandalism in our school?'*

3. Make a list of suggestions (students enjoy this part!), eg: *provide free paint; remove all opportunities for self-expression in lessons; deny students individuality; make no effort with school décor; provide nothing to do at breaks/after school...*

4. Turn the suggestions back to positives, generating ideas and triggering new ones, eg: *create a graffiti wall; invite graffiti artists in to give lessons; staff and students to explore contentious issues together and perhaps represent in pictures; encourage strong sense of personal identity; provide students with choice in lessons...*

Talking about creative thinking

Language to help your students talk about their experiences might include:

> generate   develop   adapt   refine   combine
> transform   synthesise   blend   seek alternatives   imagine
> visualise   invent   compose   think laterally   create

Ask your students what they think about the creativity techniques:

- *'Did you find these techniques helpful or did they get in the way?'*
- *'Can you see a use for any of the techniques in other subjects or in the real world?'*

Other possible talking points:

- *'What does 'being creative' mean?'*
- *'What does it feel like?'*
- *'Can you be creative in any subject?'*
- *'What helps you to be creative? What makes it hard to be creative?'*
- *'What could your teachers do to help you become more creative?'*

Evaluation

Where's the problem?

> *Evaluation is superficial – little awareness of the criteria they are using to judge value of work or ideas.*

Students don't always appreciate the importance of criteria in making judgements; why they might be necessary, or how they can be used and misused. They are often unaware of the criteria they are using in their everyday lives to evaluate all manner of things: which team to support, which jeans to buy, which girl or boy to ask out.

Students who have formerly claimed to find evaluation 'impossible' in a classroom context, have been encouraged to have a go when they realise what a commonplace skill it really is. The thinking tools in this section can be used to make the process of evaluation 'visible' to students. These tools are:

- Diamond Ranking
- The Target Board

Thinking tool: Diamond Ranking

'What would be worse: to lose all your teeth; lose your way; lose your friends; lose your memory; lose your money or lose your temper?'

The answer to a question like that provides insights into your values and it is your values that inform the countless decisions that you make in a day.

Diamond Ranking is a thinking tool that immediately engages students in **prioritising** and helps them **analyse** and **evaluate** the criteria they adopt and apply when making **value judgements**.

Failing to 'get the priorities right' is a common cause for complaint in public and private life and, as living becomes increasingly complicated with ever more possibilities for choice, it is important that students know what is involved in making **good judgements**.

Diamond Ranking instructions

1 Take an issue relating to your present topic that invites your students to make judgements on a number of items. For instance, you could ask them to rank the importance of a number of jobs, the desirability of a range of personal qualities or the likelihood of a range of technological innovations – anything that requires judgement rather than 'correct' recall.

2 Show the Diamond Ranking template and explain the significance of the shape. The boxes are arranged in five levels of importance from the single most important down to the single least important.

3 Form groups of two or three and give out the items to be ranked.

4 Explore the differences in judgements between the groups and any differences in values that may underlie them.

Diamond Ranking template

For younger learners, you could adapt the template to create a four-box Diamond.

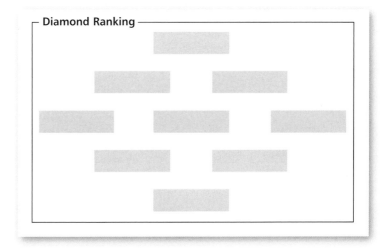

Diamond Ranking teaching tips

Lead in with a light-hearted everyday life example, perhaps introduced as a personal anecdote, eg choosing a present for a relative or friend. What would your students suggest?

Provide eight rather than nine items and ask groups to come up with the ninth themselves. This can be progressed to the point where students generate their own items entirely.

Sometimes students recognise that the order of ranking would change depending on particular conditions or contexts. Encourage students to explore these possibilities as this will lead to more flexible thinking.

The debrief will be easier if you focus on each group's top and bottom choices, asking questions that help your students uncover the criteria they used for their placement.

Diamond Ranking – talking about thinking

Words that might help in the course of the activity and in the plenary are:

rank	least	criteria	preference	
prioritise	less	equal	judgement	choice
judge	most	value	significant	order

Ask your students:

- *'How did you decide that that was the most important/significant?'*
- *'Why do groups disagree on the importance of that/those?'*
- *'What contexts did you have to agree on before you could rank the items?'*
- *'How did the Diamond Ranking tool help you to prioritise?'*
- *'When might the ability to prioritise come in useful in everyday life?'*

Thinking tool: Target Board

The Target Board can help students to develop and use criteria to **make balanced, comparative judgements**. Used to its full potential, it can also help them develop their own generalised strategy or 'golden rules' for making judgements.

Which	**hits the bullseye?**
Criteria	for making a judgement about...
1	
2	
3	
4	
5	

Target Board instructions

Decide upon your focus for evaluation. Using the template opposite, an example from a History lesson might be: *'Which eyewitness hits the bullseye?'* with the focus on making a judgement about *'reliability'*.

1 Ask students to draw up a list of five criteria upon which they will base their judgement. In this example they would be asked to describe the attributes of the *'perfect'* or *'ideal'* eyewitness.

2 Students now match each data item – in this example a selection of eyewitness statements – against their list of criteria. The target board itself also has five rings. Only if an eyewitness matches all five criteria can their name be written in the bullseye. If they fulfil only *one* criterion, their name will be written in the outside ring, and so on.

3 Students use the Target Board template to reach balanced comparative judgements. The activity draws them into making clearer distinctions between data items, leading to more nuanced judgements.

Target Board teaching tips

Model the use of the Target Board yourself with a day-to-day example such as *'Which car hits the bullseye?'* developing criteria to make a judgement about *'My ideal car.'*

Students enjoy having a go at examples such as *'Which mobile phone/ song/house hits the bullseye?'*

Target Board teaching tips

Continuing with the eyewitness example, a good extension activity is to ask your students to invent an eyewitness and eyewitness statement of their own. They must decide in advance whether their eyewitness will hit the bullseye, or miss the target board altogether. They then use the Target Board to evaluate each other's eyewitnesses and check whether they have fulfilled the relevant number of criteria.

You can expect older or more experienced students to begin to spot and push against the constraints of this particular thinking tool. How, for example, do they indicate the *relative importance* of different criteria? How do they indicate how *well* a particular criterion has been fulfilled?

Target Board – talking about thinking

Provide students with the language they will need to talk about the thinking they have been doing in using the Target Board:

criteria   **compare**   **match**   **judge/judgement**   **evaluate**

Encourage students to *generalise* their learning by setting them the following challenge:

'If a younger student needed to evaluate or make a judgement about something, what 'golden rules' would you give them to follow? Remember! Your 'golden rules' must be general: they must work for any subject.'

This will help your students to recast the steps they have taken into a more generic and therefore transferable form.

Introduction

 Processing Information

 Reasoning

 Inquiry

 Creative Thinking

 Evaluation

 The Thinking Lesson

The Thinking Lesson

From 'what' to 'how'

So far this Pocketbook has focused mainly on the 'what' of teaching thinking – the important ideas to be aware of and a series of practical thinking tools for classroom use.

This chapter offers further practical tips, but focuses more on the 'how' – the 'craft' of teaching thinking. It will help you get the most out of the tools offered in previous chapters.

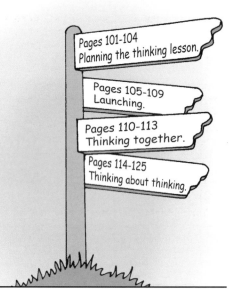

The 'learning zone'

With careful planning, *every* lesson can help to develop better thinking. As with all skill development, your students' progress will depend on your appreciation of their present skill level and your understanding of what they should be aiming to do next – under your guidance.

If the thinking is too easy, then they may find your lesson boring and do nothing to improve their abilities. **Too hard**, and they may give up entirely or rely totally on you – and again nothing useful will be learned.

Between the two lies the 'learning zone', or as Soviet psychologist Lev Vygotsky termed it, the 'zone of proximal development'. Here:

* You challenge your students to think just beyond their present capability, with you at their side to encourage and guide
* Your students learn new skills and gain confidence as independent thinkers

The 'learning zone'

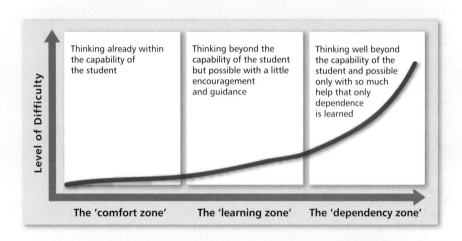

Thinking already within the capability of the student

Thinking beyond the capability of the student but possible with a little encouragement and guidance

Thinking well beyond the capability of the student and possible only with so much help that only dependence is learned

Level of Difficulty

The 'comfort zone'   The 'learning zone'   The 'dependency zone'

The perfect challenge

Vary the degree of challenge to match the capabilities of your students, by taking into account the following criteria of progression:

Nature of stimulus

Familiar	Novel, unfamiliar
Concrete	Abstract
Single aspect or small number of steps	Multi-dimensional, multi-step

Type of thinking

Relatively easy focus, eg sorting	More complex focus, eg evaluation

Language for thinking

Simple terms that connect ideas	The language of more complex reasoning

Degree of scaffolding

Step-by-step guiding	Open-ended method
Use of thinking frames	No frames, or student-designed frames
Regular teacher mediation	Students mediate for each other

A meal in three parts

Imagine a thinking lesson as a three-course meal. All three courses are carefully planned using selected chunks of curriculum content infused with thinking skills.

Part 1 - Launching

Appetising openers that stimulate the need to know.
(pages 105-109)

Part 2 - Thinking Together

Open to a variety of tastes and providing plenty for our customers to chew on. (pages 110-113)

Part 3 - Thinking about Thinking (Metacognition)

To aid digestion and complete the experience.
(pages 114-125)

Setting thinking objectives

Most teachers share objectives with their students. These may be subject specific teaching objectives or learning objectives. In a lesson designed to encourage better thinking in any subject area, it is helpful to share the intention to focus on one particular thinking skill and aim to improve it.

Thinking is always about *something* and so it makes sense to link the thinking skills objective to a subject specific objective. For example, in an English lesson, the aim might be to improve the skill of **making inferences** as well as to **deepen understanding of a character** in a play. This could result in the following learning intention:

*'To be able to make **reasonable inferences** about Macbeth's state of mind at given points in the play.'*

Identifying what you know with 3, 5 & 7

If learning is a journey, then we will want our students to be skilled navigators in what may be, at times, difficult waters. Begin by 'pushing the boat out' and quickly 'getting them on board' so that they know what kind of thinking they will be doing, why it matters and how they might be doing it.

The first minutes of the lesson are also a time to 'raise the issue' and connect them to what they already know and feel about it. A strategy for doing this is **3, 5 & 7**:

- On your own: write down **3** things you remember about our current issue
- With a partner: combine your ideas, lose one or remember new ones so that you have a list of **5** things about the issue
- And if time permits and the students are enjoying it: combine pairs and agree on **7** things you remember about the issue

Identifying what you feel with FeelyGauge

Emotion and motivation are words to do with movement. We feel 'moved' and as a result 'make moves' to find out, discover and achieve things.

'FeelyGauge' is a simple strategy for helping students to identify their feelings about a topic, feelings that will provide the push that launches their journey of discovery.

Make a set of FeelyGauges like the one on the next page. Prepare in advance three questions that probe feelings associated with the topic. If, for example, the lesson will focus on the ethical issues surrounding face transplantation, the questions might be:

1. *'How do you feel about donating your organs?'*
2. *'How would you feel about someone in your family having a face transplant?'*
3. *'How would you feel about donating your own face?'*

Using FeelyGauge

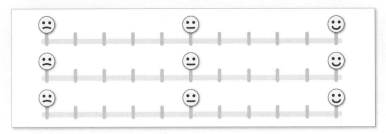

1. Have the students place a 'tiddlywinks' counter at the centre of each of the three lines and ask them to place their forefinger on the top one.

2. Ask the first question and encourage your students to slide the counter to the point, between the two extremes, that indicates their feelings.

3. Repeat for the other questions and then encourage students to **compare and contrast** their responses with a partner and put a name to each feeling. This encourages them to consider **differences in nuance and intensity** and to develop a wider 'emotional vocabulary'. They can record their 'emotion words' on a large wall version of the FeelyGauge.

Creating a need to know – 8Q

Sometimes students don't have an emotional connection to a topic because they don't know much about it. That's when you have to create a 'need to know'.

Film clips, newspaper articles, photographs and 'shocking statistics' can all provoke feelings of puzzlement, annoyance or intrigue that can lead to students asking the questions that will stimulate their thinking. 8Q is a simple strategy that supports the formulation of these questions using the template below.

Paste a relevant picture/ piece of text here and ask students to write in their questions prompted by each of the 8 question stems.

Who...   What...

Should...   Why...

Could...   When...

How...   Where...

The most interesting questions can be offered to a class 8Q, and the most promising of these can serve to stimulate an inquiry.

Exploratory talk

Thinking in the **middle phase of the lesson** is collaborative and is usually, but not exclusively, achieved through talk. Students will express views, give reasons, challenge views and come to agreement. They do this through a type of talk that may well be unfamiliar to them: **exploratory talk**.

Exploratory talk involves critical but constructive exchanges between speakers. Statements are offered with the expectation of challenge but challenges are justified and alternative ideas are offered. The competition is between ideas not individuals, so changes of mind do not mean loss of face. The chief characteristics of exploratory talk are:

- Longer exchanges
- Contributions that build on previous comments
- Giving and seeking reasons
- Speculation

Talk rules

Exploratory talk is difficult and rarely happens without deliberate coaching on the part of the teacher. Establishing 'talk rules' helps. These can easily be agreed by groups of students sorting a set of suggested rules under the headings 'helpful,' 'unhelpful', 'possibly helpful' and then agreeing on the final set as a whole class.

Such a set will include obviously helpful rules, eg *'Keep to the agreed topic'* and, *'Only one person talks at a time'* as well as unhelpful ones, eg *'Don't get involved so you can't be blamed if you are wrong'* and, *'Criticise people for making mistakes'*.

The set should also include some examples from a grey area where students will tend to disagree with each other, will have to justify their ideas, negotiate and reach a consensus. Examples here might include: *'There should be a leader who makes the decisions'* or, *'Don't listen to people if they are confusing you'*.

Question prompts

Exploratory talk can be further supported by using prompt cards during discussion.

What do you think?	What are your reasons?	Encouraging the giving and seeking of reasons
I agree with you because...	I disagree with you because...	Encouraging contributions that build on previous comments
Is there another way of looking at this?	What if?	Encouraging speculation
Have we considered all the factors?	What have we agreed?	Encouraging negotiation, collaboration and consensus

With **inexperienced learners**, each student in the group can take it in turn to ask another student a question. The whole group then listens to the response. With more **experienced learners**, prompt questions can be presented on a place mat kept on the table as a reminder.

The 'guide on the side'

Golden rules for teachers in the 'thinking together' stage are:

* Watch and listen to the group work, making notes that will inform the metacognition stage that follows
* Intervene as little as possible so that the students can learn from their collaborative attempts to succeed
* If you do intervene, do so as a coach rather than an instructor. Telling them what to do may ensure they get a solution to their problem but it will lessen their capacity to think for themselves. Getting them to identify precisely what the problem is generally stimulates their suggestions for ways forward

Metacognition

We learn a lot by watching, imitating and adapting what we see. Imagine learning to dance when the dancers around us are all invisible. Thinking is invisible.

The plenary in a Thinking Skills lesson is distinctive because it puts thinking under the spotlight. Students are asked to share not only what they have learned about the subject, but also what they have learned about the process that made the learning possible, ie their thinking. They are also encouraged to think about how they might use their thinking skills both across the curriculum and beyond, into everyday life. We call thinking about thinking **metacognition**.

Metacognition requires lots of support and the quality of your questioning and listening will be key to its success.

Rich questioning

You can develop your students' ability to think metacognitively by asking 'rich' questions. They are rich because they can draw out a wealth of possible responses regarding knowledge, know-how, thoughts, feelings and speculations.

Being a rich questioner involves you in asking questions about things you cannot already know the answer to, questions about how your students think and feel. Don't expect an immediate reply to your rich questions; give students time to think.

Listen closely to their responses so that you can:
- Ask follow-up questions that challenge and extend their thinking even further
- 'Join up' their thinking so they can learn from each other

The ASK model

We find it helpful to think of learning as a development of **A**ttitudes, **S**kills and **K**nowledge (ASK). As well as providing a structure for planning 'well rounded' lessons, the ASK model can help you to structure rich questions:

Skills
Processing information
Reasoning
Inquiring
Creative thinking
Evaluating

Attitudes
Critical
Reasonable
Open minded
Persistent

Knowledge
S=d/t
Terminal moraine
Causes of WW2

Display an ASK poster on your wall to remind you and your students what learning is all about.

ASK about Attitudes

Questions linked to students' **attitudes** will explore the **learning dispositions** that motivate and sustain good thinking. Examples include:

persistence	determination	curiosity
open-mindedness	flexibility	showing empathy
taking responsible risks	striving for accuracy	finding humour
courage	friendliness	honesty
patience	reflectiveness	posing problems
questioning	applying past knowledge to new situations	

Examples of **A**-rich questions are:

*   *'How did your feelings change in the process of tackling the task?'*
*   *'What personal qualities enabled you to think well as a group?'*
*   *'Why do you value that?'*
*   *'Imagine you had faced that problem on your own. What would have been your attitude then?'*
*   *'Which disposition were you most tested on?'*
*   *'How did you overcome the problem?'*

ASK about Skills

Questions linked to students' **skills** can explore their thinking skills as well as their subject-specific skills.

Examples of **S**-rich questions are:

- *'How did you go about doing the activity?'*
- *'What type of thinking were you doing?'*
- *'Can you give an example of this?'*
- *'How did you know you were thinking well?'*
- *'Why did you reach that conclusion? Yes, but how is it that your decision is different to that of the other group?'*

Try using sets of 'word cards' to help your students develop the language they will need to think and talk about their thinking and learning. You will find example vocabulary accompanying each thinking tool in this Pocketbook.

ASK about Knowledge

Questions linked to students' **knowledge** can simply reinforce the subject specific knowledge they've gained in the lesson or they can help to transfer a developing thinking skill to its application in other contexts. (For more on transfer, see page 123.)

Examples of **K**-rich questions are:

* *'What knowledge did you draw on to be able to do this task?'*
* *'Knowing that... how will it help you at home?'*
* *'What is the value of knowing that?'*

Phrases for thinking

Try providing your novice students with an ever-increasing set of phrases via wall displays and placemats that will support their exploratory talk. Examples are:

- *I think...because...*
- *I agree with...because...*
- *I disagree with...because...*
- *Another reason is...*
- *This is the same/similar/different because...*
- *This is as/less/more/most important because...*
- *If...then...*
- *First we...and then...and finally...*
- *This is better/worse than... because...*
- *An alternative might be...*

Talking about thinking – some activities

Create a set of 'skills' cards and 'attitudes' cards using the example words accompanying each thinking tool in this Pocketbook.

Give each group of students an identical set of cards – not the whole pack, just four to six cards showing the types of thinking (or the dispositions) that you planned to focus on. You could also include one or two cards showing a type of thinking that they are unlikely to have used – as a red herring.

The activities on the next page show how you can use the cards to get your students talking about their thinking and learning.

Talking about thinking – some activities (continued)

1 How did you go about doing the task? Pick out the cards that show the kind of thinking that you were doing. Can you give an *example* of when you were doing this kind of thinking?

2 Can you sequence the cards to show the stages that your thinking went through? What did you do first... and then..?

3 Try to agree on which was the *most important skill* (or disposition) that you needed to do the task.

4 Select a card showing the skill (or disposition) that you found the *easiest*.

5 Select a card that shows the skill (or disposition) that you found the *hardest*. Why was it more difficult? What helped you to rise to the challenge?

6 Select a card with a 'thinking word' that was *new to you* today.

The problem of transfer

The transfer of learning is widely considered to be a fundamental goal of education, yet it is also one of teaching's most formidable problems. Research shows that students typically show little ability to apply what they learn in one curriculum area, to help them with a new and different problem in another. Knowledge and skills that could be generalised and transferred, remain stubbornly welded to the context (and sometimes even to the room!) in which they were learned. They are still less likely to be applied to the solution of informal problems in everyday life.

It is important to acquaint students with the whole problem of transfer, and show them **how to learn for transfer**.

One prerequisite for the successful transfer of learning appears to be the extent to which students have developed the tendency to metacognitively monitor their own thinking. Have your students learned to ask themselves the following questions:

'What's this about?'; 'How shall I do this?'; 'What have I done before that might help'?; 'Where could I use this again?'

Transfer strategies

You can help your students to develop metacognition by modelling the type of reflection required and by **asking questions to promote transfer** before and after an activity. Using the sets of vocabulary cards mentioned earlier, you could ask questions to cue both 'backward-reaching' and 'forward-reaching' transfer.

Backward-reaching transfer

- *'Select a card that shows a type of thinking that you have used before in other lessons'*
- *'Can you explain what you were doing?'*
- *'How might this skill or strategy help you with this new task?'*

Forward-reaching transfer

- *'Where else might you be able to use these skills?'*
- *'Select a card that shows a type of thinking that you can see might be useful in a different lesson or outside school'*

Transfer strategies

As well as identifying the particular thinking skill or disposition they have been developing, students also need to reflect on its **value** and to consider where such a skill or disposition might be **useful to them again**. Two game-show style activities that students enjoy and that promote this kind of reflection are:

WTP ('What's the point?') Following an episode of collaborative thinking, conduct a WTP challenge for one of the skills or dispositions that have been identified in the plenary. Backed by some suitable game-show style music, give the class one minute to figure out the value of say, 'persistence, or 'making connections'.

11/21/41 (or '8/18/38' or '16/26/46' depending upon the age of your students!) Students are challenged to come up with a convincing reason why a particular skill or disposition is useful NOW when they are 11; might still be useful when they are 21; and might still be valuable when they are 41.

7 golden rules for making thinking important

1 **Create a climate for thinking** – Model your own desire to learn about your students and your subject. Encourage them to be supportive of people and critical of ideas. Make it all right not to know and even better to question.

2 **Make thinking challenging and fun** – Plan open questions and challenging tasks that invite a variety of responses from multiple points of view.

3 **Plan for thinking** – Audit the types of thinking in your current lessons using PRICE. Plan in more 'thinking lessons' infused with thinking skills.

4 **Organise for thinking** – Organise your room to encourage collaboration and dialogue. Allow your students time to think before responding to questions and provide them with time to think metacognitively at the end.

5 **Evaluate thinking** – Engage your students to reflect on the variety and value of their thinking and the strengths and limitations of using 'thinking tools'.

6 **Make thinking visible** – Display thinking words, thinking phrases, question prompts, thinking tools, the ASK model and the thoughts of your students.

7 **Make thinking audible** – Think out loud to model the steps; ask rich questions; teach exploratory talk; encourage dialogue. Listen with care!

Resources

Activating & Engaging Habits of Mind
by A. Costa & B. Kallick. Association for Supervision
& Curriculum Development, 2000

Critical Thinking for Students
by R. van den Brink-Budgen. How To Books Ltd, 2000

**How to Teach Thinking and Learning Skills:
A Practical Programme for the Whole School**
by C. J. Simister. Sage, 2007

Models of Learning: Tools for Teaching
by B. Joyce, E. Calhoun and D Hopkins.
Open University Press, 1997

Probing Understanding
by R. White and R. Gunstone. Routledge Falmer, 1992

Six Thinking Hats
by E. de Bono. Penguin Books Ltd, 2000

Teaching Children to Think
by R. Fisher. Nelson Thornes Ltd, 2005

**Think it – Map it! How Schools Use Mapping
to Transform Teaching and Learning**
by I. Harris and O. Caviglioli.
Network Education Press, 2003

Thinking for Learning
by M. Rockett & S. Percival.
Network Education Press, 2002

Thinking from A to Z
by N. Warburton. Routledge, 2000

The Thinking Through Series
D. Leat (series editor). Chris Kington

Thinking Through School
by A. de A'Echevarria and D. Leat.
Chris Kington, 2006

**Words and Minds: How We Use Language
to Think Together**
by N. Mercer. Routledge, 2000

About the authors

Both Anne and Ian are directors of the educational consultancy, 'Thinkwell'.
Its enquiry-led professional development programmes in thinking skills, creativity,
enquiry based learning, EI, coaching and leadership have international standing.

Anne de A'Echevarria

Anne established Thinkwell in 2007. Before this she was a youth worker in
Paris, a teacher in the UK and France, a PGCE tutor and, in association with
Newcastle University, helped to establish 'Thinking for Learning', a research
and development team based in the North East. Her interest in creative
writing and education combine in her use of storytelling to lead innovation
and change, and in the creation of stories to foster student enquiry into
learning. A recent example is the award-winning Thinking Through School.

Ian Patience

Ian's long-standing interests in education and art have led him to work as
a stained glass window maker, a mosaicist, an illustrator, a fine artist and a
teacher. A belief in the value of creativity lies at the heart of Ian's work. He
encourages teachers and students to enjoy challenging accepted norms
and to feel confident in constructing new and better ways of living and
learning.

Contact Anne and Ian at: www.thinkwell.org.uk